A Book About the Water Cycle

Water
Is Water

Miranda Paul   Illustrations by Jason Chin

A NEAL PORTER BOOK
ROARING BROOK PRESS
NEW YORK

For Baptiste, Soleil, and Amani
—M.P.

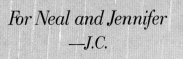

For Neal and Jennifer
—*J.C.*

Drip.
  Sip.
Pour me a cup.
Water
    is
       water

unless . . .

it heats up.

Whirl.
Swirl.
Watch it curl by.

Steam is steam *unless* . . .

it cools high.

A dragon
    in a wagon?
A crow
    kneading dough?

Clouds are clouds *unless* . . .

they form low.

Misty.
Twisty.
Where is the town?

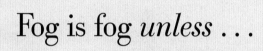

Fog is fog *unless* . . .

it falls down.

Patter.
Splatter.
What is that sound?

Rain is rain *unless* . . .

on the ground.

Slosh
    in galoshes.

Splash to your knees!

Puddles are puddles *unless* . . .

puddles freeze.

Glide.
Slide.
Put on the brakes!

Ice is ice *unless* . . .

it forms flakes.

Pack.
Stack.
Shape it and—

—smack!

Snow is snow *unless* . . .

spring comes back.

Creep.
  Seep.
Squish in your boots.

Mud is mud *unless* . . .

there are roots.

Swig.
Grow big.
Reach for the best.

Apples are apples *unless* . . .

they get pressed.

Drip.
Sip.
Pour me a cup.

Cider is cider . . .

until we drink up!

More About Water

Water moves and changes often—just like children! Also like people, each drop of water travels its own unique path. This story shows only some of many creative ways that water moves and changes over the seasons. Although the characters in the book sometimes heat up, drink, or play with water, nature usually moves and transforms water all by itself through the **water cycle**.

 In *Water Is Water*, a cup of water begins its cycle as a **liquid**. But then:

It heats up: The white swirl that rises above a boiling pot or cup of cocoa is still water, but we call it **steam**. It will become an invisible gas in the air. Did you know that the Sun, not people, heats up most water (without forming swirls of visible steam) and turns it into a **gas**? Whichever way it happens, this process is called **evaporation**.

 It cools high: As an invisible gas, water is called **vapor**. Once vapor reaches cooler air, often high in the sky, vapors form **clouds**. This is called **condensation**.

They form low: When water vapor cools and condenses close to the ground, the clouds that form are called **fog**. Fog is not as common as high-flying clouds and plays a very small part in the water cycle. Bus drivers must be thankful for that!

 It falls down: Once water droplets inside any cloud become too heavy, they fall down as **precipitation**. Though rare, water droplets in fog can drip or drizzle down, but most precipitation comes from higher clouds. Whenever water falls down from clouds as a liquid, it's called **rain**.

On the ground: Water that moves on top of the ground is called **runoff**, which often collects in puddles, lakes, rivers, and oceans.

Puddles freeze: When the temperature drops below a certain point (32° Farenheit, 0° Celsius), water turns into its **solid** form, called **ice**.

It forms flakes: **Snow** is made in the sky when bits of ice form **crystals** around specks of dust or pollen. As they fall, vapors freeze and stick to each crystal to make flakes.

Spring comes back: When temperatures warm up, the **snowmelt** runs off into streams and rivers. Along the way, some water mixes with dirt to make mud!

There are roots: **Seepage** happens when water creeps down from the top of the dirt into small spaces underground. When plant roots **absorb** this water, it's called **uptake**. This helps them grow and produce fruit.

They get pressed: Although apples are **solid**, the water inside makes them plump and juicy. Squeezing them releases the liquid.

We drink up: Did you know that *you* are mostly made up of water? "Drink up" water every day to stay as amazing as you already are!

A baby is about
78% water.

An apple is about 84% water.

Earthworms are
about 80% water.

Water is . . . everything!*

A garter snake is
about 74% water.

An oak tree is
about 75% water.

A turtle is about
70% water.

You are about 65% water.

A cat is about
80% water.

percentages by weight

Water is . . . everywhere!

Water covers 71% of the Earth's surface.

Of all the water in the world, oceans hold 96.5%, which
is all **salt water**.

Of all the **freshwater** in the world,
more than 69% is trapped as ice and snow,
and 30% is underground.

All the water in the clouds, puddles, mud, plants,
and your cup doesn't even add up to 1% of our total
freshwater supply.

Water is . . . important!

Water may seem to appear and disappear, but the total amount of water on Earth hasn't changed in millions of years and will stay the same for millions more. Although water changes form and gets called by different names, new water is not created and old water is not destroyed. But that doesn't mean we should take water for granted. In fact, people can only drink way less than 1% of the water on Earth. Almost every time we use water—to brush our teeth, take a bath, or flush a toilet—we add things that make it dirty. It is important to **conserve** it so there is safe, clean water for everyone.

FURTHER READING

Green, Jen. *How the Water Cycle Works*. New York: PowerKids Press, 2008.

Jango-Cohen, Judith, and Tess Feltes. *Why Does it Rain?* Minneapolis: Millbrook Press, 2006.

Lyon, George Ella, and Katherine Tillotson. *All the Water in the World*. New York: Atheneum/Richard Jackson Books, 2011.

Morrison, Gordon. *A Drop of Water*. Boston: Houghton Mifflin, 2006.

Woodward, John. *Water*. New York: Dorling Kindersley Limited, 2009.

SELECT BIBLIOGRAPHY

Bastin, Sandra, and Kim Henken, Eds. "Water Content of Fruits and Vegetables." University of Kentucky College of Agriculture, December 1997. www2.ca.uky.edu/enri/pubs/enri129.pdf.

Bell, Trudy E. *Science 101: Weather*. Irvington, New York: HarperCollins, 2007.

Hall, Stephen E., Ed. "A Summary of the Hydrologic Cycle." WW2010, University of Illinois. ww2010.atmos.uiuc.edu/(Gh)/guides/mtr/hyd/smry.rxml.

National Oceanic and Atmospheric Administration. "How Do Snowflakes Form? The Science Behind Snow." December 21, 2011. noaa.gov/features/02_monitoring/snowflakes_2013.html.

United States Environmental Protection Agency. "Drinking Water & Ground Water Kids' Stuff." water.epa.gov/learn/kids/drinkingwater/index.cfm.

U.S. Geological Survey. "The USGS Water Science School." water.usgs.gov/edu/.

ACKNOWLEDGMENTS

Thank you to Howard Perlman, U.S. Geological Survey, for valuable insights on
the scientific technicalities of water and the water cycle.
I would also like to acknowledge Katie Collins Garrett, meteorologist at the National Oceanic and
Atmospheric Administration and climatologist Ryan Boyles for their expert reviews of some of the
explanations in this book. Further credit goes to Dr. Stephen Secor,
associate professor at the University of Alabama, and Brian T. Henen, PhD,
for providing some hard-to-find statistics.

A Neal Porter Book
Published by Roaring Brook Press
Roaring Brook Press is a division of Holtzbrinck Publishing Holdings Limited Partnership
120 Broadway, New York, NY 10271
The art for this book was created with watercolor and gouache on paper.
mackids.com

Library of Congress Cataloging-in-Publication Data
Paul, Miranda.
    Water is water : a book about the water cycle / Miranda Paul ;
illustrated by Jason Chin.
        pages cm
Summary: "A spare, poetic picture book exploring the different phases
of the water cycle in surprising and engaging ways"— Provided by
publisher.
    ISBN 978-1-59643-984-9 (hardback)
1. Hydrologic cycle—Juvenile literature. 2. Water—Juvenile
literature. I. Title.
    GB848.P37 2015
    551.48—dc23

                                                                    2014031493

Roaring Brook Press books may be purchased for business or promotional use. For information on
bulk purchases please contact Macmillan Corporate and Premium Sales Department
at (800) 221-7945 x5442 or by email at specialmarkets@macmillan.com.

First edition 2015
Printed in China by RR Donnelley Asia Printing Solutions Ltd., Dongguan City, Guangdong Province

13 15 17 19 20 18 16 14